T0208616

Reclaiming National Sanity

Our Nation Under God

R.M. Trowbridge, Jr.

iUniverse, Inc.
New York   Bloomington

iUniverse books may be ordered through booksellers or by contacting:

iUniverse
1663 Liberty Drive
Bloomington, IN 47403
www.iuniverse.com
1-800-Authors (1-800-288-4677)

Because of the dynamic nature of the Internet, any Web addresses or
links contained in this book may have changed since publication and
may no longer be valid. The views expressed in this work are solely those
of the author and do not necessarily reflect the views of the publisher,
and the publisher hereby disclaims any responsibility for them.

ISBN: 978-1-4401-6796-6 (sc)
ISBN: 978-1-4401-6795-9 (ebook)

Printed in the United States of America

iUniverse rev. date: 09/22/2009

Foreword

The purpose of this book is to show *precisely how to reclaim sanity* in our nation through principle adherence application. On a wholesale basis, millions of individuals have reclaimed sanity by that method, and so can our nation. The reclamation process is strictly voluntary and cannot and will not be forced on anyone. The trick is to do it in your own way and in your own time, but do it. In this work, *Our Nation* refers the environment, and *Under God* are the principles.

Our nation began with a manifesto. *Manifesto* as defined by Webster is: "A public declaration of intentions or principles esp. of a political nature." That manifesto was *One Nation Under God*, with God as the ultimate authority above all else and principles first and a political nature second. Principles are concrete, where as politics are abstract. The Constitution, written for We the People, granted We the People access to those principles endowed by our Creator, those principles being laws that govern. The writers of the Constitution were into the spirit of cooperation, not the spirit of control. They were Christian men with Christian values and vision. [Washington's vision can be read at: http://www.soul.org/Legend2.html]. They were not unlike ourselves as modern Americans, with various occupations, political views, social enjoyments, religious backgrounds, and economic status. They had rebellious natures and were not going to be dictated to or controlled by government—any government, even the one they were forming. They were considered radical, rebellious, non-compliant rebels by outsiders and onlookers. They shared a common bond and togetherness without laptops, cell phones, iPods, or Twitter. They created a formula for a new nation upon which all could absolutely agree, and all signed it. Existing among them were camaraderie, fellowship, friendliness, and understanding, which had to be indescribably wonderful. They were willing to place principles first before personalities, yielding the outcome to God, and to die for them. This meant that our leaders were there to serve but never to govern, similar to the principles of servant leadership where leaders use their power to empower others (we the people) instead of their own positions (the government). The government will not be the papa that will bail you out. The papa of the government will bail you out. *God* is papa. The truth is papa.

If We the People are truly ready to get off the merry-go-round we all are riding on—manufactured by a government of individuals seeking governing control that has been established and is deeply rooted and always looking for the bigger, better deal—and replace it with a government of individuals seeking to serve, then a radical reversal will be necessary. A complete and total reversal of direction and thinking must now proceed by way of our electoral process in upcoming elections. Our founders, being Christian men with Christian values, chose God-centered, Christ-centered laws—honesty, purity, unselfishness, love—and placed these laws, precepts, and principles at the head of the table. These laws were to govern. These men truly loved God with all their hearts, all their souls, all their minds, and all their strength, and their neighbor as themselves, forming Our One Nation Under God for We the People.

Our nation, our government, is not a religious organization; it utilizes precepts common in all religions yet has no affiliation with any. It includes Catholics, Protestants, Jews, Hindus, Muslims, and Buddhists.

This is not a book about philosophy but a book regarding self-observation and practice that produces change and which practices are needed for a specific change. I am attempting to show that *honesty, purity, unselfishness, and love,* or *dishonesty, impurity, selfishness, and unlovingness,* are principal practices in daily affairs, not just intellectual philosophies.

A brief synopsis for reclaiming sanity follows:

1. Recognize the need for change due to unmanageability

2. Decide to adhere to the regenerative life

principles and surrender the results of that practice over to God

3. Amend damages done by past degenerative practices where possible, stop the current degenerative practices, and be accountable for doing so

4. Continue to practice the regenerative principles, asking for help from our higher authority (God), and immediately set right any wrongs that may occur

5. Help others who want to adopt this manner of living in their personal life and in their service to the government

This work is presented more as an outline rather than in story form, based on personal and other stories to illustrate points regarding principle practices.

I am attempting to show that if a person practices degenerative principles prior to assuming a leadership position in government or in personal life, then the government will inherit those same principle practices, not just babble. When people babble, they talk about that which they are not doing. If you do it, you know it, the principle that is, and if you don't do it, you babble about it. The babbler never sees themselves as a non doer. The mirror thing again. For example, if you believe it is okay to cheat prior to leadership, then you will practice cheating during leadership. The same is true with the other principles, such as impurity, selfishness, unlovingness. I have found that credibility is not established by intellectual knowledge of principles but the practice of those principles, which reflect knowledge. Intellectual, degreed knowledge is good; however, if unapplied it is only babble, not credibility. All of us can talk a good game. What we get is manifested as a result of applied regenerative or degenerative principle or law practices. (I'll talk more about these very soon.)

My anecdotes reflect my immaturity with regards to the importance of honesty in living. I would rather shoot rabbits than discuss how I could be applying honesty with the Uncle Abe story.

When individuals are doing the next right thing, their morals are good and they are being honest, pure, unselfish, and loving, thereby practicing the regenerative principles, fulfilling the spiritual nature of "love thy neighbor as thyself," and all is well.

When individuals are doing the next wrong thing, they are being immoral, practicing dishonesty, impurity, selfishness, unlovingness—the degenerative principles, which are strictly self-centered, not involving your neighbor as a consideration at all. It is only the "what's in it for me" and "to heck with others," but I must make it look like it is in their best interests and the best interests of the country. This is where the liar appears, attempting to convince others of whatever, using his own brand of rose fragrance deodorant to spray over the manure. Basically it is individuals looking for the bigger better deal selfishly, for themselves only, saying they are serving, when in reality they are governing. Governing equals control.

This book is about what will be needed to place Our One Nation Under God, The Good back on firm footing, regenerating her weakened strengths and healing the ligaments that bind her together in solidarity, keeping her whole and undivided, standing upright before other nations and reestablishing principles before personalities in adherence to the life powers (principles) that produce a strengthening and cleansing joy, involving all of us as participants and practitioners.

It is most important that a third party of some kind arise that will adopt the regenerative life principles for the people to choose from in upcoming elections.

Should the word *God* offend, simply substitute the word *Good*.
However, we cannot leave God out of the process.
Our forefathers knew this.
God enters anywhere you let Him in.
He never forces Himself on anyone.

Keep an open mind and set aside any prejudices for the moment, okay?

    1. Honesty
    2. Purity
    3. Unselfishness
    4. Love

The regenerative life powers (the above principles, or laws) are for all men and women, in time, all generations young and old, in time, all institutions, small and large, in time

The higher principles, or laws, are unwavering, solid, secure, and constant, irrespective of opinion, not unlike the lower law, or principle, of gravity, which is unwavering and constant as well but can be played with—until the plane runs out of fuel or the engines are fouled with geese. Then the lesser law of gravity, irrespective of opinion or the plane's occupants, *will* take over, until the skills and prudence (another law affecting outcome is called the law of prudence) of the pilot in command, skillfully saves the *lives of all*, without defying the law of gravity. Regeneration and degeneration are not involved here.

The higher regenerative laws (principles) cannot be played with. When they are, they simply turn into degenerative laws (principles).

Regenerative Laws (Principles)	Degenerative Laws (Principles)
(Principalities)	(Principalities)
Honesty	Dishonesty
Purity	Impurity
Unselfishness	Selfishness
Love	Unlovingness (hate, anger, resentment)

Producing Freedom	Strong possibility of a stay at the Many Bar Hotel
The Rose	The Manure
Yes	No

One needs to learn to call a rose a rose and manure, manure, and not confuse the fragrances.

These principles, or laws, do not leave any wiggle room. They separate the men from the boys, because it takes courage, devotion, and real guts to apply them, to recognize that half measures will not work and that there is no easier, softer way. Any attempt to cheat the regenerative principles is doomed to endless cyclical frustrations and miseries, with only temporary remissions of suffering. It would be like playing Russian roulette with an automatic.

If a man attempts to cut you off from practicing the regenerative life principles, only then be angry with him and unyielding.

These truths are self-evident.

Washington said we are a nation respective of *laws,* not of men, thusly composing our Constitution, and another prior to Washington stated the *laws* will not be changed one jot or one title.

These are universal truths affecting all lives.

All babble will never change the rules (laws or principles).
They are, however, open for discussion.

Regenerative   or   Degenerative
(powers, principles, principalities, laws)
whatever you prefer to call them

Choose

Which side are *you* on?

Knowingly or unknowing, we *all* will (self-will) play our parts based upon each individual's choice, which affects the collective members positively or negatively.

One cannot retrieve the past tick of the clock. One can only repair the choice made during the past tick to the best of one's ability, and in some cases, no repair is available. What will one choose as an individual or as a nation at the next tick of the clock: regenerative or degenerative principles?

Continued *degenerative* practices bring about a stench first—sniff, sniff, sniff—that everyone can smell. Then comes *decay* and ultimately dissolution: past cultures, societies, nations, relationships. Pick some of your own examples.

Attention is required, attention to the principles. As an exercise in my practice of attention while driving from point A to point B, I try to pay attention to the posted speed limit laws (which are much lesser laws) and notice how many times my foot was too heavy and my discipline went to sleep. I've found that when I am in a hurry to get somewhere, I make lots of errors. Not an excuse— lack of attention and discipline sometimes comes with consequences (citations). It's never somebody else's fault. It's one's own lack of attention and discipline. If I am undisciplined in attentiveness to lesser laws, what makes me think I'll be more attentive to the Higher Laws.

Lady Justice is a symbol. Due to the blindfold covering her eyes, she may not see who stands or sits before her, and she cares not. Her decisions will not respect men or women but *laws*, endowed by our Creator (regenerative or degenerative laws or principles), signified by the scales she holds. Yet, she is fully capable of smelling manure before her, hearing manure when it hits her ears, feeling manure when her feet are standing in it, and she can taste it when someone is attempting to force it in her mouth, trying to get her to swallow it. The Sword of Truth she holds is symbolic of "you shall reap your just reward" (justice) as a practitioner of the laws regarding the regenerative or degenerative principles you voluntarily choose to practice, which are spiritual in their nature and moral in their humanity. The principles are the lifeblood flowing in the veins of individuals and the life blood of Our One Nation Under God, the Good. You know, the "what's in the vessel" thing. Each individual is a vessel, exercising honesty or dishonesty from within and manifesting that practice, and unloading their individual practice onto others or our nation. The symbol is also a representation of your own instincts, intuitions, and five senses as well.

If you are past thirteen years of age and still believe in Santa Claus, I have news for you—*there ain't one*. At thirteen you are suppose to begin behaving like an adult, beginning to make choices on your own, no longer laying responsibility and accountability on mom or dad or others. The reality is that at that age, we are still too immature, and we often carry that immaturity past our teens into our twenties or even our thirties before we snap or wake up. Some carry it all the way to the marble orchard. You know, the "they will do it for me" thing, or the "it's somebody else's fault" thing. Ignorance of the law or principles is no excuse. Ignorance is not bliss.

Principles versus personalities is the basis of one's life experiences until one reaches the marble orchard. The priorities of the individuals legislating is mirrored in Our One Nation Under God, The Good, as to whether personalities or principles were placed first with regards to judgment. Remember that judgment with regard to principles is not being judgmental.

Currently the weighed-down crucible is full of manure instead of roses. She would prefer roses. The even greater news is that *she never holds a grudge. We do—she doesn't.*

Begin filling the crucible with more roses instead of manure, thereby giving her back her firm footing. *You choose.* Remember, there is no Santa Claus.

I have found that if you are an individual who waves to others with your whole hand open, with goodwill to others, you will most likely see the truth in it. However, if you are an individual who waves to others with only one finger extended, you'll miss it.

Our national situation today is like a large glass of water that's been muddied with impurities like silt and dirt. There is no clarity at the moment. However, the ancient wisdom, or axiom, "not doing is doing" applies here. When one stops adding to and agitating the degenerative impurities and leaves the glass alone, the impurities settle out, and the purity, integrity, and clarity of the water are restored. The water has not been changed—the purity has always been there. *Recovery* is established, *sanity* restored, sanity here meaning "proper balance."

On a lighter note: here's a lesson regarding honesty applied to pleasurable pastimes. Golf has taught me a great life lesson. While playing the game with others, foot wedges are not allowed, for that club improves only your position with regards to the rest of the participants and is therefore *dishonest*. I found that if I apply dishonesty to a simple game of golf, most likely I'll apply dishonesty in other areas as well. Tigers never use foot wedges, maintaining the integrity and purity of the game equal for everyone while keeping their own integrity intact, yielding to outcome. Cream *always* rises to the top. (Congratulations on winning the Palmer tournament, proving my point: a skilled practitioner of attention and discipline, yielding to outcome even when coming from behind.) The currency that captured the tournament title was not the size or depth of his pocketbook but the only negotiable currency—time and effort and principle—for a combatant.

I also enjoy golf, and I won a charity tournament for wounded warriors, held at the Cascades golf course designed by Jack Nichols. I always wanted to play that course. I had not played in over a year. Although I'll never be as skilled as Tiger, but because of no cheating, no foot wedges, no dishonesty, we are equals. I would like to play a round with Tiger, my equal, while I still have a body to play with, before my appointed time at the marble orchard. (This is only a fantasy because of the restraints imposed by my limited skills and resources. I must keep things in proper perspective.)

By the way, how many foot wedges are pacing up and down Pennsylvania Avenue?

Wasn't there something about the common welfare coming first? Sniff, sniff, sniff.

Honesty

The first regenerative life principle was practiced by a man who became one of our esteemed leaders, who regenerated and healed our whole nation, which was torn apart and degenerated by the hate, anger, and resentments called war. Although the individual is no longer with us, the embodied principles he practiced remain. Those who would say that he did not or would not walk a mile to return one penny that was not his own to keep are only the ones who themselves would not practice that first precept, or principle, and return that which was not theirs, perhaps later giving it to someone else, saying, "Look how good I am". Sniff, sniff, sniff.

One penny or one trillion—it's not the amount, it's the principle.

Honesty begins with self-awareness. Most people's journey toward self-awareness starts with denial. They recognize the negative behavior of others and find fault with them, only because they subliminally recognize these faults in themselves. Just as Caliban in Shakespeare's *The Tempest* becomes angry when he sees his face in the mirror, so do people react when they recognize their own faults through the acts of others.

Remember that when people point their fingers at another person, there are *always* three fingers pointing back at them. The mirror thing, a subtle form of murder by character assignation, demonstrating a diva-centered life style while proclaiming one's self-righteousness.

Honesty never chooses a person, and honesty never remembers you. *You* must remember honesty; *you* must choose honesty. This requires attention and discipline, with one's self and with others, not unlike observing speed limit laws, which are lesser laws with lesser consequences, although sometimes the fruit from someone's family tree may fall prior to its ripening and appointed time, their pursuit of life, liberty, and happiness extinguished.

I remember well when *dishonesty* (cheating) crept into my life unobserved, leaving its imprint of guilt behind within. I looked over the shoulders of my classmates during test times in high school, slipping around and sneaking off, behaving immaturely and stupidly, knowing it was wrong (which was the pricking of conscience endowed by my Creator being ignored), seeking shortcuts to success and happiness (the cheater's way) while telling no one. The earliest beginnings of degenerative principle practices were going unchecked, and I believed the old-fashioned values were not modern and therefore no fun as I ignored the rules. My own laziness abounded in both areas, mental (unthinking, mental laziness) and physical (undisciplined, no self-restraint). If discovered, I blew it off and justified (another form of dishonesty) my actions, saying "others do it too" or "it's no big deal," or I blamed others using the words *but* or *because* a whole lot, absolving myself of any accountability. I almost turned it into an art form. I'm glad I wasn't good at it; too many people get hurt. However, this was also when my spiritual and moral debt was beginning to mount up, and later in life, the bill came due. Ignorance is no excuse. Ignorance is not bliss.

The individual to whom I refer above was very steeped in spirituality and equality and practiced the principles prior to his leadership role.

The principles placed him there—not promised babble.

The principle brought about change—not babble.

Lincoln (Honest Abe) led our country, which had two currencies at the time. The Union's paper money was just coming out and being printed, replacing gold. The South had its own currency as well. He would not allow adulteration of the Union's established values, thereby keeping *purity* (the second regenerative power, or principle) intact, while unifying our torn country and healing her wounds, thereby keeping love (the fourth regenerative power, or principle) and brotherhood intact while practicing unselfishness (the third regenerative power, or principle), which is placing what is right and true in every situation above individual wants.

It began with honesty (the first regenerative power, or principle). Honest Abe applied honesty—he did not always get his way either.

Thank you, Uncle Abe, for being such a good teacher and practitioner of our country's most valued assets (principles), spiritual in their nature, moral in their humanity, that can cleanse and strengthen each of us, individually and collectively, to our personal and collective health, sustenance, and joy.

Our nation is becoming a very ill patient. The patient need not be held to blame, nor the physicians who have been prescribing the wrong medications, even though they may be very well-intentioned. The *recovery* of the patient is at stake. A good beginning would be to stop taking the degenerative pills (principles) and switch meds to the regenerative pills (principles).

When a patient is thirsty, dreaming about water, or thinking about water, or even reading and talking about water, are not enough. The patient must drink and swallow the water. Take and swallow the regenerative life power pills (principles) *daily*, as best you can. To swallow means to practice.

No one is still living to verify my Uncle Abe's journey to return one penny, thereby practicing honesty, which also touches purity, unselfishness, and love. Uncle Abe had absorbed those principles prior to his leadership role. He read the Good Book daily. From it, he took the principles and applied them to daily living while becoming an attorney and then applied them as an attorney in his practice of law.

So, Uncle Abe, I know you are pleased that our nation, which you served so well in the spirit of freedom, honors and celebrates your birthday. It saddens me, however, that our one nation has kicked to the curb the one day enacted by you as a national day of thanksgiving and prayer, thusly kicking to the curb the higher principles you placed at the head of the table of honesty, purity, unselfishness, and love, which you were honoring and such a good practitioner of, in spirit. It appears that today's servants and leaders are more interested in the penny than the principles. I personally enjoyed seeing the drawing made by one of your guests of one of your evening parlor parties in the White House with your friends of the day. You know, with one of your friends perched on the piano. That was really cool. No impurity here. It strengthens and confirms my personal beliefs, even though I was not here yet. I'll leave it to the clueless researchers of today to figure that one out. There are so many prejudices existing today. Nevertheless, after dinner, while you and your friends of the day were enjoying a spiritual high, enjoying spiritual freedom, joyously dancing and singing that evening, the piano, with the friend on it, and a few of your friends in the room were levitating. Not exactly walking on water, but pretty close … As for today, if you and some of your friends were to move your monument one way or the other about six inches, today's individuals would not believe that either—there's no one to interview. It would give a wakeup call, though.

As for myself, I remember my grandmother (whose maiden name was Hanks) telling us at our family gatherings on Thanksgiving and Christmas of our relation to Abe (by marriage, not blood). My older sister Arleen remembers it as well. Both of us are still living. But as for myself, I was more interested in shooting rabbits on the farm than honesty. My later life exhibits the truth of this, which was a mixture of regenerative and degenerative principle practices, of which most were degenerative. Fed up and disillusioned, wanting off the merry-go-round (not unlike our country today), I bumped into an old man, T.E.P., and others (they know who they are) who told me, "There is no need to be fed up or disillusioned; simply change what *you* are doing." I was thirty, and T.E.P. was in his sixties then. He told me to practice honesty, purity, unselfishness, and love to the best of my ability, read the Good Book, and pray (simply ask for help even if you think nothing is listening) for the wisdom to see the truth, the will to act upon the truth, and the strength to stand fast on the truth. My Uncle Abe was a skilled practitioner of those precepts, laws, or principles, whatever you want to call them, and was mocked in the newsprint of the day, which depicted him as a monkey in cartoons. Prior to meeting T.E.P., I was the guy who would drive through the burger place, give a person $5 for the food, receive $7 in change because the person thought I gave him a $10 dollar bill. I would say nothing and drive off, under the illusion I was the winner. Oops—my own unobserved *dishonesty.*

Our government needs to stop driving off with our money. The principle is the same. It degenerates our country's integrity (strengths) and the integrity (strength) of the individuals who are implementing the policy by the practice of laziness and dishonesty. When integrity (strength) is lost, decay begins and establishes its foothold. Simply observe it. As for myself, a few weeks ago I drove through the bank, cashed a check for $600, examined but did not count the cash I received. I got to my sister's driveway and counted out $550, thinking I was short $50. I drove back to the bank, told the teller (Naoma) of the error, and she sent the $50 back to me. I got back to my sister's and was exiting the car when I saw the missing $50 bill that had dropped on the floorboard. Now I had $650. I drove back to the bank again and returned the $50 with my apology. No one knew of this event except me and the teller. This is verifiable because the people are still living. My Uncle Abe had to use his ankle express. The practice of honesty does not make me a good man. It does, however, demonstrate that when honesty is practiced, then purity is involved, along with unselfishness (placing what is right and true in a situation above what I want), and love (brotherhood) is involved as well.

Everyone knows right from wrong deep down. Had I kept the $50 and told someone, "Look what happened to me, they made a mistake." or "They are a large institution and can afford it, or they will just write it off" (my own brand of rose fragrance deodorant sprayed over the manure of dishonesty), then the friend would say, "It's not right." Then, were I to go back and return the money, that would only be an outward admittance of wrong-doing and setting it right would be practicing *humility*, not *honesty*.

Honesty always precedes discovery by others of one's dishonesty.

One last example from my own experience …

We are not doormats … you know, the "don't tread on me" thing.

I marketed my home for sale. A buyer appeared, a contract was signed. At closing, the survey accompanying the contractual sale provided by the buyers was inaccurate. The buyers said they would sue if I did not close at the time specified, according to the contract. For me to close in accordance with the contractual deadline and with the inaccurate survey would mean I would have been in violation of state law with regards to the survey boundary and subject to state law violations, which could mean state jail time and any other penalties and city code penalties, fines, et cetera, which I did not fully understand or even know about at the time of my decision not to close. I only knew the survey was wrong and things were not right at the time of closing, and I chose not to close based on the unselfishness principal (placing what is right and true in every situation above what I want), thereby touching honesty as well. I did not want to be sued. I was sued. The buyers were just trying to slip one by me. This does not mean anyone was a bad man. Mediations have been held, and my property is no longer contractually tied up and is currently for sale again.

Remember the DON'T TREAD ON ME banner?

The principles are simple but not easy. Be prepared for some useful suffering and even greater hardships while building an even greater internal strength by placing a childlike trust in the principles first, even when fearful and/or angry; yield to outcome. Don't tread on my principles. This just demonstrates that the principles hold up under fire, always. That does not make me a good man. The principles are good.

When I discovered I was being sued, I told one of my friends, Noel G., what was happening, and his advice to me was simply, "Don't lie." Remember, it's not about you, nor about pleasant or unpleasant feelings, or even how you are perceived by others, good or bad. It's about principles. Don't lie, even if you think cheating (lying) would improve your personal position.

There is my Uncle Abe's *honesty* again.

There are other men and women (like the twenty-one-year-old Ms. California) practicing the principles openly daily. They know who they are, and they are FOXy people.

So, to the lawmakers and legislators in our halls of Congress, I can only suggest that you as individuals adopt the higher regenerative laws (principles) of honesty, purity, unselfishness, and love—spiritual in their nature and moral in their humanity—as your code of conduct, placing nothing at the head of the table except these principles upon which your decisions are made, thereby making all men equal. You know, the "all men were created equal" thing, which does not mean all men are equal, because each man and woman has different talents. Equality upheld is fulfilling the Constitution, which it is your sworn duty to uphold, based upon principles for Our One Nation Under God, The Good, giving liberty and justice for all within the spirit of freedom. Ignorance is no excuse. Ignorance is not bliss.

Another thing T.E.P. said to me with regards to the regenerative principles was that if you sincerely begin doing them, you know them and the difficulties associated with them, and if you are not doing them, you only know about them. *Knowing is doing*. Knowing them intellectually and not doing them is merely arrogant babble to appease onlookers and appear great, for self-gain only. There's no strength there to stand on. Babble is easy; doing is not so easy, requiring attention, discipline, and patient practice in all of one's affairs.

So, gentlemen and ladies, as our embodied leaders, who act on behalf of our embodied nation, it would be advantageous, while each of us still have bodies to act with prior to our appointed time at the marble orchard, to place the regenerative principles back at the head of the table while we still have bodies to apply those principles with. As our nation's leaders, the decision is yours. The good never forces itself upon anyone. The bad never forces itself upon anyone. The effect of bad choices does, however, in the form of wars, unstable economy, strained relations … and the list goes on, from which we are all to protect ourselves. *Choose*: regenerative or degenerative principle practices. It's too late when we have no more breath left in us. No breath, no life, no *choices*. This is simply an observable fact.

Time to move on with a story about myself.

As a young boy—I was about fifteen years old at the time—I was on a Boy Scout trip at the nation's capitol, with the Eagle Scout merit badge dangling on my chest, standing on the steps going up to Congress. (I have photos somewhere.) I had no idea, not even a clue, as to what was going on there, or its values (principles). One could safely say my mother earned the merit badge, which she pinned to my chest at a ceremony. Again, I was clueless, young, and immature. I remember also the time my mother, while doing the books for our family's business, was reviewing the books a second time before filing the tax return. I asked her what she was doing, and she replied, "The books do not balance; they are one penny out of balance, and I'm looking for that penny." She later told me she found the penny and then filed the tax return. I was still a young boy and clueless, and I know without a doubt I would never have looked for one penny. True story. I would not have valued the principle. I never asked, but I wonder if Uncle Abe's story influenced my mother. I think yes.

Today, in my sixties, I know its value, even though I have been a very slow learner, beginning when I was thirty, when I first began to practice principles and swallow the regenerative pills for my personal life, yielding to outcome. I am still a poor practitioner, as my friends know.

Here is another example—but first a question: Is double-dipping into the funds of others (We the People) honest or dishonest?

Currently on the books, a bill passed by Congress will abolish the Death Inheritance Tax, eventually to our posterity. Isn't there something in our Constitution with regards to our posterity?

Now, another proposal added to a current bill before Congress would increase and reinstate that inheritance tax.

Question: Is a special interest group being served here, like the government or governing authorities, or is the principle of honesty being served, or is a foot wedge, so to speak, being applied because they can and are standing over the ball?

Have We the People not already paid tax on that capital earned by the sweat of our brows to dispense as we see fit to our posterity, or even *unselfishly* to the posterity of others within our one nation and her posterity? The bank, a special interest group (government?), needs more money now, like a spoiled irresponsible brat, to assist in current or upcoming bailouts imposed on its parents We the People, and We the People are powerless to influence their decision, good or bad, until the next election. Like LBJ once said, sometimes we are like the jackass in a hailstorm, just having to stand there and take it.

Our currently not-so-trusted servants have a good opportunity to recover trust by basing their decision, or vote, upon the third regenerative life power principle, or law, of unselfishness (placing what is right and true in every situation above what I want) with regards to We the People, thereby touching honesty, purity, and love (brotherhood) and placing those principles at the head of the table above special interests.

Remember, it's not about the money or even the amount, it's about principles. We all need money to live and cannot get around it. It's not about destroying money, only destroying the image in the money, that image being that money will fix everything. It does have its comforts, though. I like money too.

Principles are laws that govern.

To each item contained in a bill, apply the acid test. Is each item honest or dishonest, pure or impure, unselfish or selfish, loving or unloving? Does it hurt anyone with regards to our nation or We the People? Have the strength (integrity) to stand on those principles and delete the degenerative and keep the regenerative, yielding to outcome, regardless of personal or special interest influences in the daily matrix of our existence.

Simple, but not so easy. Devotion to the principles takes real guts. This is diving into the liquid of *liberation*. Who was it who said, "Give me liberty or give me death?" Patrick Henry. Did he know what he was talking about, or what? Remember the twenty-seven year-old Iranian woman who was shot in the chest, blood running from her nose and mouth just prior to taking her last God (Allah) given breath? God is God, or breath is breath, in any language. See yourself. Roll the tape. Our leader would not even send one bandage out of "Love thy neighbor as thyself." Instead, he had the backbone of a jellyfish. Our leader, while abroad representing our nation, pointing his finger back at our Nation saying we are not Christians while having three fingers pointing back at himself. The mirror thing. Himself placing abstracts (politics) first and concrete (principles) last. A wishy washy display of character if you ask me. Our Nation's leaders are using pennies as bullets toward "we the people" and cannot see it. You decide. A decision is choice. By the way, a decision not to decide, is a decision.

The regenerative or degenerative principles, or laws, are not up for review—*we are,* as practitioners of those principles which our founding forefather so devoutly cherished (loved). These principles were here prior to my birth and theirs and will still be here after my departure and will always be with us and posterity.

Our founding forefathers fled the tyranny and oppression imposed by earthly kings and dictators and rulers in order to serve something far greater than men and more enduring. They choose principles or laws to govern men, thereby forming an environment to establish our Constitution for We the People. True knights, serving something far greater than themselves, with even less reward and even greater hardships, not thinking of their comforts in order to pass it on to posterity (those who were to follow after their passing). As Washington said, referring to our nation, we are respecters of laws (principles), not of men, knowing we could not force others to do likewise, either outside our borders or inside our borders. You try leaving your warm cabin and crossing the Delaware in the dead of winter to protect our principles within our borders while practicing the principles. I'll bet not just the crop but the entire farm that most, not all, would choose something more comfortable than an open boat. Hurray for the practitioners forging through the cold, foul, wet weather for the Tea Party. I like comfort too; the question is, am I willing to sacrifice my cushioned comfort, whatever that may be, and endure the discomfort and sufferings that arise from placing what is right and true in a situation above what I want? As for myself, I was living in Hankins, New York, on the Delaware with my friends

Mickey and Bob during December, in eighteen-degrees-below-zero weather with a blizzard blowing. Mickey had a severe crick in his neck, causing pain and suffering, and we could do nothing. We called Tom, (T.E.P.),who lived about three miles away, for help at 1 am. He left his warm comfort and came, not thinking of any reward to himself, and he stayed two hours and relieved Mickey's suffering. Tom was a good practitioner of the third regenerative life principle, or law, of unselfishness.

Don't let the word *knighthood* put you off. It simply means to do the next right thing and live your life that way, without quitting or selling out. We all are combatants. They, our founding forefathers, with courage, devotion, and guts, dove into the liquid of liberation, forming Our One Nation Under God, The Good, serving the principles, not the comforts or likes and dislikes of men. Let those who have eyes to see, see. Principles first, to the best of one's ability, and The Way will meet you, lead you, and support you.

Hurray for Ms California, who stood up unyieldingly for *purity*. When asked about sexual relationships, she responded with a male-female relationship answer—sexual purity. Just prior to her answer, she interiorly sought counsel from the Most High and received her answer, placing what is right and true in every situation *above* what she wanted: the *unselfishness* thing again. Remember the saying "Does anyone ask and not receive?" Remember the "one nation under God" thing, or on our currency "In God we trust" thing. The twerp asking the question, who would be promoting *impurity* later, took out his aerosol can of rose fragrance deodorant, spraying over the manure, publicly saying she could have given a different answer, thereby self-justifying (a form of dishonesty) his righteousness to himself and others. Sniff, sniff, sniff. He had other choices also, but he did not ask interiorly for counsel. He could have torn up the card and asked a more appropriate question and chose not to do so, only demonstrating his lack of guts regarding regenerative spiritual principles, or laws, spiritual in their nature and moral in their humanity. There's an empty vessel for ya, at that tick of the clock, making noise, having no marketable goods on board or inside, but with an okay paint job, grinning before cameras, standing on sand. I personally know individuals who have totally and permanently reclaimed sanity from such a malady, which verifies to me that their condition is a voluntary personality pleasure preference not unlike tobacco users, yet more complex. Both conditions are amendable where proper balance can and has been restored. Reclaiming sanity begins by wanting it first. Legislatively speaking, the smokers cannot impose themselves on non-smokers. Federal law, I think, supports purity of breath. Great job. Have we gone the other way now with regards to sexual purity, and federalizing sexual impurity? I know I'm stupid in some areas; however, I don't think I have succumbed to being the village idiot just yet.

Thank you, Ms. California, for being such a good ambassador of the Most High under which all of us live and move and have our being, and Our One Nation Under God, The Good, proving my point. Your tiara is the far greater Starry Crown. The Absolute (the Executive and Sovereign Monarch of the Universe) did not bow or yield to anyone, took what came, and blamed no one, as you took what came and did not yield to anyone or blame anyone. *No empty vessel here.* You are one who can take a pledge and be allegiant to her betrothed and Creator, who will also be able to take a pledge and be allegiant to whomever you may choose to marry. I hope that whomever that person may be will provide a firm footing for your feet to rest upon, with or without trimmings, while you *unselfishly* maintain and lovingly tend your magnificent home for posterity. Wow.

Also, thank you, Sarah Palin, for being such a good practitioner of the regenerative life principles in thought, word, and deed, and your daughter for her recognized youthful immaturity and change of heart, thusly practicing sexual purity in thought, word, and deed as well. You have a great daughter there. Wow.

Moving on now to the Navy Seals pirate thing—Good call, good counsel. There's that unselfishness principle again. Number 44 has the right to bear arms and has a huge warehouse full of them for use at his discretion against invaders of our posterity's properties. Should we expect less for ourselves individually from our leaders, who may attempt to control or remove our rights to bear arms and protect our individual posterity's properties against invasion by the practitioners of the degenerative life principles? Control or removal of the right to bear arms is not an affirmation of *equality*.

This is a nation respective of laws, not men. Washington, what laws could our founding forefathers have been referring to?

There were no tax codes, no social security, emission laws, et al., back then. Could it have been the regenerative laws (principles) endowed to each man from his Creator? I think yes.

The Principle of Nature = Natural Law
The Principle of Gravity = Physical Law

Nature cannot examine itself; however, man with a natural body can while he exists in nature. If man stays asleep, he has no recognition of a need for change and no examination of his life or our nation's life (present current condition), which is currently the reflections of practitioners of the degenerative principles, although claiming otherwise. There are those who are practitioners of the regenerative principles, like the intelligence agencies and Newt and many others who are keeping us honestly informed, even with the dirty little political game-playing, keeping the secrets as they should (secrets are good). Thank God (who we are under as a nation, remember) for such men. Those men—we should wash their feet and like it. I know I would. But if we are going to just hope for the best based on old ideas and what we believe is okay and expect different results, it won't happen—the different results, that is. We will be like the Ostrich with its head buried in the sand and its rear end getting battered around, denying the problem or hoping it will change by itself. Our wrong belief has done us in, not our lack of faith. Different weapons will be needed that are connected to their source, which are ancient yet modern; dust them off. Our skills will be resharpened.

Our old mortal weapons, the "more money will fix it," or "the institutions will fix it," or "bigger and better rehab centers or more psych meds will fix it," or the " we have a pill for that" fix-it syndrome, must be let go of absolutely. We must recognize that *we are in serious trouble, very, very serious trouble.* We are going to have to find some immortal weapons somewhere that really do care if we live or die as individuals and as a nation. Imhotep sure doesn't (from the movie *The Mummy* with actor Branden Frasier). Right now, we have more plagues than you can shake a stick at, and they ain't leaving voluntarily. Just look at the dishonesty on the floor of Congress, that lady caught up in lies, and her well-intentioned friends saying "hang in there," but they will sell her out while professing otherwise. Not unlike Imhotep wanting the girl to go along with him, saying he will spare her friends. When she goes along and he has what he wants, he turns and says, kill them all. Remember Beni in the movie? I liked Beni; he chose sides too and thought he would be immune. Look what happened to Beni. Ancient yet modern. Maybe not just a fairy tale ... It speaks more to the truth than fantasy, and you intuitively and instinctively know it, in your gut. We must now turn back to our Source— you know, the "Under God the Good" thing—pick up some of the immortal weapons, like honesty, purity, unselfishness, love (the regenerative Principles, or powers, or laws), raising us up, killing the bad guy. He can and will do it based upon our choice. Emanuel, God, is here is with us, We the People, One Nation Under God, the

Good. We just need to get our little finite rear ends into action and reconnect to the infinite. He can make chicken salad out of chicken s--- (manure).

Get ready for a fun date, and to take some hits. It will not be boring, dull, or glum. Bring along your sense of humor because it will come in handy too. Humor is the antidote to the venomous anger of others. Are you going anywhere? This can be fun—serious, but fun. There's no Santa Claus, but there is a Creator. Welcome to the real NFL: no free lunch. Even the water boy is a combatant. All of us will get a new high, nonchemically induced, recognizing that the spiritual principles are vocally kicking a----(rear ends) and not our physical appendages, but empowering our physical nature to vocally kick a—(rear ends) where needed and at the right time and in the correct manner, not too much and not too little.

Poverty is the worse form of cruelty. One must make the injustice visible and be willing to die like a good soldier in order to do so. Expose the degenerative principle practitioners. Rats are always the first to leave a sinking ship; they intuitively and instinctively know a storm is coming. The rats with the biggest tails are getting all the syrup; the money?

Currently, California is bankrupt, and our nation is headed there as well, producing more national poverty. A new third party of some kind must come into existence, whatever you want to call it, delivering all of us under the oppressions of our current parties that are so deeply entrenched. Government today is more focused on the penny, not the principles. This new party should be devoted to the principles first, serving the underlying spiritual nature, or precepts, thereby serving the higher part of ourselves, the invisible parts containing the power and not our physical existence that is *mortal* and temporary, whereas the spirit is immortal, like unto the soul. Our forefathers knew these truths and placed principles before personalities. We do not see them as self-evident today; we unknowingly and uncomprehendingly voluntarily disconnected, whereas they did not, recognizing a higher authority, the spiritual that is hidden underneath the physical. Washington and all those men served this knowingly and comprehendingly, with fellowship. Their lives were spiritually based, where as our lives are materially based. They had conscious contact; we lost ours. They had no doubts, no lack of faith with regards to the principles; we do. If we do not first see it, we do not and will not believe it, because we want proof first. Our lost conscious contact with these truths placed us all in servitude to the physical over the spiritual.

This is why a new party of some kind will have to emerge, placing principles before personalities if Our One Nation, Under God, the Good is to be healed more quickly. Put the regenerative principles (spiritual in their nature) back to first and the physical will follow; the physical world has to yield because the physical world has no will, remember. Our forefathers had lots of fun whoopee parties; they kicked asses and were not boring, dull, or glum and were very happy, yet devoted to the principles first, knowing psych meds won't get you there. Thank God, they did not have them to do battle with—placing their hope in meds. They had different battles: forming a Constitution for One Nation Under God, the Good. They had the wisdom not to attempt to regulate or control perversions that existed and were practiced in their time as well. They were aware of them, and to say otherwise would be foolish. They wisely left perversion issues up to the individual and left it up to individuals to work it out within their individual consciences, with their Creator, or they would have written it into the Constitution as well. They had higher wisdom; we muddle around in lower wisdom. Christian wisdom transcends philosophy as grace transcends man.

This new party would have to commit to no more bailout money, not one penny; also to look at gay and abortion rights and make a decision on those; to open the waterway to California's crops and let God take care of his fish. Stem cell researchers can go to a surviving good bank for money and not the government. Energy companies can go to surviving good banks for money and not the government. We need a party committed to getting the government out of the money-lending business, totally committed to less governmental control in business areas. That is something the individuals will have to decide for themselves. The above are basic suggestions.

This reminds me of a story of one of my friends, an attorney, by the way. Not unlike myself and others, having reached the fed-up-and-disillusioned stage of life, he wanted off the merry-go-round, went out and purchased a gun, went to the hardware store and got a rope, went to the gas station and purchased some gas, then went to the drug store and got some arsenic pills. He drove to a bridge, climbed upon the railing, tied the rope to the bridge and the other end around his neck, poured the gas on himself, took the arsenic pills, pulled out the gun and put it to his head, lit the gas and jumped, pulled the trigger. He shot the rope, fell into the water, extinguishing the fire, swallowed water and threw up the pills, hollering for *help*. Remember, God loves life, your life, and it ain't over until He says it's over. So he thrashed around, hollering for help, and a boat came by. Pulled inside the boat, he looks around and notices the others in the boat. All of them have charred britches too. They share the regenerative life principles (spiritual in their nature and moral in their humanity) and say "Do this instead. The suffering is up to you." Today, he is one of the happiest, most joyous and free individuals I know, with the same living problems the rest of us have. He too had to *choose*.

Our nation is one huge boat carrying lots of charred britches. We the People would have to start a third party, distinctive in its acceptance and practice of the regenerative life principles (laws, precepts, powers), whatever you want to call them, to the best of our abilities, forming a fellowship, helping and serving one another selflessly, joyously, placing the principles up front before personalities. The Creator has provided many good men to choose from to lead and would humbly realize that they are not the power, only the servants, and temporarily at that. Go for it! When the students are ready and willing, the teacher, who will not be some dingbat or idiot, will appear. That individual will appear by way of the spirit's choice and the spirit of truth—the infinite's choice for its beginnings of reconnecting to its Source.

When the regenerative principles are up front, then one is not going to be far off the beam. Mistakes will be made, and the stubbing of toes will happen, so be prepared for that, but you won't be far off the beam, and it can be amended as soon as recognized. It will take about a year and a half of time, effort, and principle adherence before one will begin to see the evidence, and three years before there will be no doubts. This principle follows the law of three, which I will not go into here, but which I have applied and experienced. This bird being still young may not be ready to fly yet. That's up to the Creator, but it will fly.

The principle of honesty = law
The principle of purity = law
The principle of unselfishness = law
The principle of love = law

Principles are laws that govern.

The above principles are constant, with us prior to birth and remaining after our passing.

They cannot be legislated by any body of men anywhere nor forced onto anyone; each must choose to yield to them and apply them each moment in the arising situations. This is not a theory but an observable fact.

We as men and women can create a lot of human conduct laws.

However, we as men and women cannot create:

    natural laws

    physical laws

    honesty laws

    purity laws

    unselfishness laws

    loving laws

Creation of the laws is over; it's done.

Creation is done and is good.

We as human beings can *only* play with them, which we are doing, in our One Nation Under God the Good, endowed by our Creator. Hello! The Constitution thing …

So, it appears we have done it to ourselves by our own choice. Now we must voluntarily yield to the higher regenerative principles (laws, precepts, values, whatever you want to call them) or suffer the consequences of continuing to practice the degenerative principles expecting different results. To me, that's *insanity*.

Let us not forget: the principles bow to no one.

The absolutes of those principles:

Absolute honesty

Absolute purity

Absolute unselfishness
Absolute love

The Absolute did not bow before Pilate because he was under God, the Good, and Christ did not apologize for anything nor condemn (point fingers or blame) anyone.

The Absolute, the Exemplar of the foundation of Our One Nation Under God, allows human beings to pass on to our posterity, as the Absolute in living flesh passed on His posterity—all of us.

Remember these sayings?
"Without me was not anything made that was made."
"Before Abraham was, I *am*."
"I *am* with you always."
"If you do not believe in me, believe in what I do."

How about the real simple one: "Follow me"? It was not a request, it was a command (Oops. I personally missed that part early in life), more than just a good idea that's optional for spiritual freedom, redemption, and saving our nation, religiously termed salvation. Washington wrote the following from his vision, "Let every child of the republic learn to live for his God, his land, and the Union."

We as individuals are not Absolutes, and cannot be, so don't look for perfection from me and I shall not look for perfection from you. But we can and are to follow the Absolutes as closely as humanly possible, given our individual situations, until we reach the marble orchard. It is the choice of each individual or collective of individuals in our Congress. I will, however, look for right effort on your part, and you should expect the same from me.

The men forming our Constitution knew these spiritual truths and practiced them to the best of their ability during their time in time. We must pick them up, placing principles first before personalities.

Regenerative or Degenerative Principles

I write these things with a loving heart and not with any malice toward anyone. I do not wish in any way to offend.

Learn from the mistakes of others. I have found others to be good teachers. I personally have had to learn from my own mistakes, correct them and amend them, observe and listen to others so I would not have to experience some of their mistakes. Others, having different warts than myself, have been some of my greatest teachers, if I did not focus on their warts and did focus only on what they were trying to tell me. Each person individually has to personally deal with their own warts if they are to grow. That does not mean I have to yield to their warts for people-pleasing purposes. Wisdom has the humility to seek and ask for help.

The laws of nature gave number one through number forty-four and each man a mansuit to wear at birth. This does not mean I am a man. What is inside the suit determines manhood: principles—honesty, purity, unselfishness, love—developed interiorly by intellectual remembrance of those laws, disciplined practice, and placing the principles first and absorbing them in the heart, which develops one's character and integrity (strength) within, which is "to thine own self be true,"—not the wishy-washy character that is blown about by the winds of change and circumstance, with lots of mind changing going on, which is ego-based.

Remember, it is the emptiest ship or vessel that makes the most noise.

You cannot transmit something you do not have.

The lower legislated laws of men protect us, believers and nonbelievers, from the practitioners of degenerative principles or laws. Practitioners of dishonesty, impurity, selfishness, unlovingness (hate, anger, resentments) who threaten to come down on others to get their selfish needs fulfilled are wrong.

Choose the higher laws, individually and collectively as a nation.

Our nation has gone back to sleep, steeped within its comforts, placing comfort first instead of principles. It's time to *wake up*.

Remember Yamamoto's vision after hearing of the dishonesty executed by their ambassador in Washington, DC:

"I fear we have only succeeded in awakening a sleeping giant."

We the people are that giant. We can do it for ourselves, as my Uncle Abe said.

Right now, the giant sleeps. *Wake up!*

When the idiot realizes he is an idiot, he is no longer the idiot.

When one is having or living in a bad dream, simply wake up. The bad dream disappears, but not the memory of it or the experience of it.

Each person is also a sleeping giant. Remember the saying, "He that is within you is greater than he that is within the world." My uncle Abe (by marriage, not blood) said something along those same lines when he said, You can do it for yourselves.

Principles are laws that govern.

We are the posterity of the privileged, with or without trimmings, and currently *blowing it.*

We argue about the fleas and ticks irritating the lion and are so focused on the ticks and fleas that we no longer see the lion. We (the people) need to decide (choose) which is more important: the life of the ticks and fleas or the life of the lion.

Pick the ticks and fleas:

The following ticks and fleas are sucking the life out of the lion and laying their eggs.

Taxes: promoting special interests bailouts

AIG: bailout monies

Car companies: bailout monies

Governing authorities with special interests first, professing otherwise

Gay rights, based on personality preferences not regenerative principles

Abortion rights, based on personality preferences because of individual:

Laziness, lack of discipline and self-restraints coupled with lack of:

Knowledge with regards to dynamite (a new life) and playing with dynamite as though it were a stick of candy. Ignorance is not bliss.

No respect for the dynamite, only a taste for candy. It is very dangerous and unwise to kick sacred things around. They have flashing signs saying, Warning, Warning, Warning, Hot Plate, Burn, Burn. We say to ourselves, we are smarter, more intelligent and can ignore the rules. Oops. (I will talk of this very soon.)

Remember, it's never too late. Time and mercy are not out of our reach until we reach the marble orchard. *Time is our enemy, not our friend.*

There is the "we do it to ourselves" thing, wanting someone else or Santa Claus to fix it.

A short story about myself ... Born of privilege, I'd reached the fed-up-and-disillusioned stage of life, not unlike our nation's dilemma today. I bumped into the regenerative life powers or principles when my sister Arleen called back home to our mother and said, "Don't give him another penny for the rest of his life." Well, Mom did it; she *cut me off.* Upon reflection, it was the best thing that could have happened to me, although at that time I sure did not think so, and it did not feel good either. I was forced to pick up the regenerative life powers and principles and apply them, not knowing what the outcome was to be. It was my first experience with having to place trust in the principles. It worked. Later, Mom set up small trusts for her grandchildren, to be used for education purposes only, as her posterity, with a specific clause in her will that stated that none of the monies in trust were ever to be spent as bailout money for any difficulties they got themselves into. It worked. All her grandkids are solid. The principles worked. That's my personal experience, with no bailout money, ever, and I am still here and okay.

Are you ready to spell *fun* backwards now? Had nuf? Ready to holler *Uncle* yet, proving it by amending amendments, putting in your 1 percent of time, effort, and principle?

He, the Creator mentioned in the Constitution, will provide the 99 percent needed, knowing you cannot do it by yourself, and will always meet your efforts more than half way because of his love and mercy. Not my rules, his rules. The pure and the impure will never mix. You can make a mixture, but it will settle out. You can never make an emulsion. You cannot fool the Creator. He knows the length of your hairs and when you got your last haircut and the intent of your heart and is even closer than your very breath. He never gives you any more than you can handle, and He is definitely no fool who can be conned, like doing the same old things, expecting different results. Our Creator loves all the lives he has made and is most definitely not a joy killer.

Radical changes will be needed; your sincerity will be tested by actions (faith without works is dead), amending amendments, before you are looked at differently and taken seriously by our Creator. Remember, if you believe this, then belief is the blossom; the action is the faith bringing forth the fruit that will feed all, We the People. Remember, the "keep it simple, stupid" thing: KISS. The best ideas are simple ones based in humility. I personally do not have a whole lot of that, as my friends know and will tell you. If you want to know me, just ask my friends who know me. If you ask me, I'll immediately start lying.

I just mentioned belief (blossom) and faith (fruit), which are spiritual qualities to all. One does what one believes, which produces fruit (via faith). Faith is constant, always there, not unlike the law of gravity, both being invisible.

Yet the results are visible to the human eye. Faith is constant, while beliefs vary. The higher invisible law of faith is connected with our spiritual nature and our moral humanity. Beliefs vary, while faith does not. Faith does not mean which church I attend. An example: say, you, the man, are a good ole boy who is having a bad hair day or a bad week and is being a real A-hole for that week. Your significant other has the meals prepared and jokingly says if you don't quit being such a jerk and stop abusing the privilege of being one now and then, you may just find some arsenic in your potatoes, and you both just crack up laughing, exercising your belief. You know her and her good will and good nature, and she would never do such a thing, so you just eat the potatoes and all is okay. Later in the week, you are eating potatoes with another meal, and you find yourself dead. What killed you? Was it your lack of faith or wrong belief? You exercised faith by eating the potatoes, so it must have been your wrong belief that did you in. If you attend church services, by all means continue to do so regularly and drink from His cup by practicing the regenerative life principles or laws as best you can.

Belief and faith are exercised daily in all sects, denominations, organizations, and institutions that have a spiritual nature or connection that's not religious. It is not hard to understand. It's spiritual, making it universal law as well. The word *religion* comes from two Greek words meaning to bind back together the ligaments. That is the spiritual meaning. Our nation today has weakened ligaments because we have eclipsed or kicked to the curb the Creator of our existence, the "Under God, The Good," by ignoring the principles and loosing our spiritual connection with and knowledge and understanding of its importance. Ignorance is no excuse. Ignorance is not bliss. Wrong beliefs have brought us and our country to where it is by the practice of the degenerative laws, or principles: by believing in personality promises instead of principles first in our highest positions. So, no wonder the Supreme Court and lower courts and Congress merely make judgment rulings with regards to personality pleasure preferences and who can produce the best babble (arguments). The babbling parties never see or connect to the higher regenerative or degenerative laws, which are spiritual in their nature and moral in their humanity, which our founding forefather were serving. The giant sleeps—there is no awareness or awakening bringing us back to our source, individually or collectively, by way of practical reason. Practical reason is now only one-sided because of our lost connection to that source, the "Under God, The Good" thing, the Creator mentioned in our Constitution, thereby serving personalities either knowingly or unknowingly. Personalities are great as long as they are not bent.

My own personal experience, having totally and permanently reclaimed sanity with regard to sexual impurities (loose morals, cheating while married, and cheating while not married—meaning sex outside of marriage as a single man)—had to stop, even though it was only on infrequent occasions). I have no desire to go back to those old degenerative practices of my ignorant youth. I fully realize that gay and abortion rights that were legislated, attempting to ease the conscience of impure sexual practitioners, is merely legislation with respect to men or women's personality pleasure preferences, whatever the cause, which is a whole different topic, thereby eliminating their personal struggle within themselves to clean up their own act. You know, the pumpkin heads streaking, running about with their light on but nobody is home. Like the empty vessel thing. Total self-absorption with no external considerations with regards to others. Individual conscience is a blessing, endowed by our Creator to each individually, spurred by guilt (the guardian of each individual's sanity). The fact is that some men and women succeed in killing their conscience and do anything they like and feel no qualms. They have so denied and trampled on conscience, perhaps weak in the beginning, that it finally subsides, thereby making them free and powerful in their degenerative practices, and of coarse quite crazy.

Oh yeah, the sex issue—well, here goes. The word sex comes from the Greek word *sacrum*, which means sacred. Men possess Zoe I and Zoe II, the life force. Women possess the sacrum, the cradle of life, which brings living spiritual souls, with no rear ends yet, from beyond the blue of the sky and from beyond the stars to take on rear ends, your rear end. (Are you still with me here, or are you measuring me for a white dinner jacket with long sleeves that tie behind my back and calling for a big nurse?) The process we all know about. We are unable to see the invisible part of the process, but the woman intuitively and instinctively knows without seeing, especially when the dynamite goes off and changes from candy to dynamite. No small thing. This is a universal thing, not just the property of sectarians and bigots. Still with me? Well, here comes the nuttier part. You would have to see Blake's portrait of "The Grave" to follow this next part spiritually. Blake drew the soul leaving the man's body, what we call death, and the soul is female. The man has a masculine body, giving him his masculinity, while the soul gives him a loving, caring, understanding, gentle spiritual nature as well, from within. If kept in proper balance, he won't be shaving his legs or armpits, thereby maintaining proper balance and therefore maintaining *sanity*. For the woman it is opposite, giving her the ability to nurture and provide for the young, and if the guy decides to go out for a loaf of bread and never return, she has the masculine abilities within to also do what is necessary to provide both male and female duties. All of this is present in our spiritual nature, akin to our Creator. Union is loving, joyous, and sacred. Form dictates use, which is endowed by our Creator. To drive nails with a screwdriver or turn screws with a hammer would be insane, but some try it anyway. Even worse is the fact that some even hand down rulings in favor of insanity.

Now we are back to conscience, endowed to each of us by our Creator. What aids and assists us in the killing of conscience when we are behaving badly and we feel bad or guilty? The three most-used substances to make conscience subside and permit the behavior are alcohol, drugs, and tobacco. We drug our conscience voluntarily, though unknowingly, so it will shut up and we can get on with the acquiring of what we want and get high and feel good the cheater's way (dishonestly). There is nothing wrong with those substances when used properly, but they do suppress conscience. When improperly used over time we deny and trample on conscience to where it subsides, making individuals free and powerful and of course quite crazy, demanding their rights from their now-bent personality preferences with no qualms. All this is spiritual in its nature and moral in its humanity. When legislation is passed as respecters of men or women, the legislation sucks our nation down into the vortices of the impure practitioners with regards to promoting personalities instead of laws endowed by our Creator to We the People. This is amendable. The degenerative practitioners are going to do it anyway and don't need a document granting permission. You know, the pumpkin head attempting to suck down Ms. California nationwide with regards to sexual impurities.

Each person knows within, for conscience was endowed by our Creator.

It will take all of us to rescue the damsel in distress (our nation), placing her back on firm footing, killing the bad guy (dishonesty, impurity, selfishness, unlovingness), saving the world. Hey, guys, everyone including the ladies gets to be the hero, and get the girl (our one nation), who maintains and lovingly tends a magnificent *home* for her posterity by way of the spirit of truth.

The recipe for reclaiming sanity is within these pages, and the only other things needed is *you,* placing the regenerative life powers, or principles or laws, back at the head of the table, placing the executive and sovereign monarch of our one nation and the universe, under God, yielding to outcome whether a believer or unbeliever. Honesty, purity, unselfishness, love.

One huge drop by our embodied leaders of the time, which is correctable and amendable, was when a law was passed removing the teachings of our founding forefathers, thusly truncating the learning and practice from our posterity, from the We the People's public schools, replacing them with badges and sniffing guard dogs. Put the principle back, recognizing a higher authority than ourselves. Even our founding forefathers recognized a higher authority and placed it up front. This one act alone will produce such a great, overwhelming change (for the good) that you, the legislators, will stand in *awe* over its effect. What do you have to lose?

In my experience, from grade school through high school, the Pledge of Allegiance was recited at the beginning of each day in school, hand held over the heart, to Our One Nation Under God. True, in those early years, my intellect was not fully developed, having no clue as to its depth of meaning with regards to serving something far greater (unselfishness) than only my personal self-interests. I did not even know what a pledge was, much less what allegiance meant, but the mature teachers knew, and the underlying spirituality of the spirit of freedom, by the mere recital of those words, were sinking in unknowingly at the time.

I enjoyed the FOXy coverage of the tea party of We the People. I observed a spiritual high produced in the spirit of truth permeating everyone present and in myself, viewing from my sister's home with joy because of its honesty, purity, unselfishness, and love. Did you also notice the nonviolent gathering of all walks of life—not one shot fired, no guns anywhere that I saw, and a *high*, not chemically induced? No dishonesty, no impurity, no selfishness, no unlovingness, no frothy anger, hate, or resentments. I only saw fed-up frustrations and anger at those attempting to cut us, We the People, off from the regenerative life principles, or laws, for We the People are currently not valued by our elected servants, who have sworn to uphold. Ignorance is no excuse. Ignorance is not bliss.

T.E.P. told me "The root trouble against which all the rules (the regenerative principles or laws) are directed is *egotism*": exaggerated personal self-sense giving rise to a condition variously termed *craving, desire, lust, thirst, clinging, sticking, attachment, infatuation, delusion, beguilement*—in English *concupiscence;* Greek *epithumia;* Sanskrit *moha;* Pali *tanha;* Russian *prelest;* modern American, "To hell with you, Jack. I've got mine."' It appears our Congressmen and women are saying, "To hell with We the People, I've got mine.

The sleeping giant is once again awakening. Stay awake.

Gresham's Law: "Bad currency drives out good currency."

One Trillion? Printed for distribution?

The established value has thusly been adulterated, degenerated by choosing the third degenerative life power (principle) of impurity, instead of choosing to practice (keep) the regenerative life power (principle) purity, in place.

Back to the regenerative or degenerative choice again.

One world currency? This would only degenerate our currency and turn U.S. currency into confetti for use in upcoming New York City parades.

Oh, aren't there some attorneys steeped in law on Capitol Hill? Check the time cards and see where they were when these decisions went down with regards to Gresham's Law.

Just because one owns the ink, paper, and, more importantly, the plates does not mean to go ahead and print and distribute more currency, simply because one can. This is like the exchanging or trading of junk bonds or the trading of worthless securities back and forth between banks and investors, with nothing of value at all. This is bad currency, and when it collapses, the good currency collapses right along with it, therefore driving out good currency. The same *law* holds true with regards to regenerative or degenerative principle practitioners voted into leadership positions. When the bad currency of the practitioners of degenerative principles (*dishonesty, impurity, selfishness, unlovingness*) with self-seeking goals is leading, usually professing otherwise, then the good currency of regenerative practitioners (*honesty, purity, unselfishness, love)* is driven out. One can plainly see that fair is not involved here. If regenerative principle practitioners are voted into positions of leadership, then the degenerative principle practitioners will run themselves out, because they do not want to change. That does not mean that the regenerative practitioners have to give in. It is more loving to stand firm.

Belief is not what you intellectually know. Belief is what you do. If I believe in something, I do it. That is my belief. I may know otherwise but not do otherwise.

The amendment process available to individual Americans by our government of the people, by the people, for the people could review the following suggestion. The current economic crisis that individual Americans are suffering due to economic collapse cannot be totally fixed. How can the government that received capital gains taxes over the years from fraudulent securities allowed to slip through the cracks of the Securities and Exchange Commission be amended to individual Americans? They (the government) can't pay it all back. Here comes the hard ball. Unselfishness (placing what is right and true in every situation above what I want) should be enacted by passing a federal law that individual personal properties that have a lien against those properties held by federally backed banking institutions on or before July 4, 2009 are now cancelled by federal law. This would be using servant leadership power to empower others (we the people). This is for individuals only, omitting no one with liens, and not for companies or institutions. True, this will not fix it, and some will benefit more than others, but a position of gratitude by recipient Americans should be adopted rather than complaint. There is no exchange of currency. This is a one-time deal only. If the individual needs to refinance, that is on them, not the government. The government will have done the best it can for We the People and then must move on. Amends completed, finished. This bill can have nothing else attached to it or to be used as leverage to get something else passed. That would only allow impurity to creep in. Now that's about principles, not money, and it is *honest, pure, and loving* as well, healing Americans as best one can. Hurting people is easy; learn to heal people. Thus, the government will have alleviated some of the poverty. Remember, poverty is the worst form of cruelty.

Gresham's Law is not a theory or philosophy or psychology. Simply observe it. Evidently here is another law that does not recognize the word *fair*. You know, the "that's not fair" thing. *Fair* is a word used to appease others, a courtesy, not law. Fair does not exist with regard to law. I have found that if I'm following the regenerative principles, I very seldom have to approach fair.

The lesser law of prudence, when given attention and rightfully applied, affects outcome with regards to Graham's Law, the same as when prudence, rightfully applied with regards to the Law of Gravity, affects outcome. The laws are unchanged.

Arrogance usually is not a good thing because it keeps me closed-minded, and that affects so many lives. You know, the "I am the president" thing. This is not saying our elected presidents are bad men. They are not. None of them. Sometimes these men act upon bad counsel

Ughhhhhhh, sniff, sniff, sniff. Panties in the White House? Ughhhhhhh, sniff, sniff, sniff. Watergate?
These were merely applied degenerative life powers (principles) of impurity and dishonesty. Those individuals occupied center stage, and that does not make them bad men. Those men are, however, held responsible for their own actions, the same as we are.

Have not we all done similar types of things at one time or another, myself included? No rock chunking here … Humility coupled with restraint has proven to be more productive. Humility, because the realization of the need for change brings one back to allegiance to the truth, the regenerative principles, awakening and surrendering to our Creator (mentioned in our Constitution), coupled with our commitment to change and cleansing via amendment of life while serving others.

National dilemma: What is it based or resting on? Lack of principle adherence. Why? What causes this inability to place principles first in the halls of Congress or even in our individual lives? The popular term is *ego*. The ego is a good thing but must be kept right-sized so as not to run over the lives of others, protecting against my self-interests at the expense of others. Ego is the lesser part of myself from which my personality functions, spinning me and those around me down into the vortices of my practices, referring to the regenerative or degenerative laws. In short, my lying self-will (actions) claims to be honest, having no idea that there is a higher I, or self, within that can stand on principles independently without regards to cost. To begin to function from the higher self is scary, and one pretty much feels alone. Therefore, the easier, softer way is reverted to, the lying self-will of personality, subtly convincing me to protect its interests, claiming that what I'm about to do is in your best interests. The liar claims to be honest. You know, the "I won't get their vote if I don't conform to their wishes, or promise them anything while stealing their lollipops," or the "I don't need to do this but they do" thing, the "let's make a deal" approach. Or how about the "everybody else does it so it must be okay," or even the "yes, I would like a new cottage somewhere, scratch my back and I'll scratch yours but don't tell anyone" thing. It's my personal self-justification (a form of dishonesty) process. My higher self observes my lower self and feels the wiggle, quickly says "Don't tell anyone," and I observe it not, never looking at it again, and move on until I'm discovered by someone else; then I start trying to clean it up and still look good. Oops.

There was a time when others wanted what we had: the principles first and a place to practice them. They wanted to be here and were willing to go to any lengths to get here. Now they only want to be here to take advantage of us. We do not even practice the principles now; thus we are in the vortices of degenerative principle practices, trying to make them work, only adding further to the confusion, lack of peace, and chaos. We *must* regain our childlike trust in the principles of honesty, purity, unselfishness, and love, spiritual in their nature and moral in their humanity, in Our One Nation Under God, the Good. The place, our nation, is only as secure as its practitioners.

We cannot change playgrounds, but we can change playmates through the election process for We the People. This will involve making radical changes with regards to the regenerative laws or principles. A fearless and thorough house cleaning could be in order here, keeping the marketable principle practitioners and the deleting the unmarketable. In my own life and my business life, I had to discard damaged goods and keep the useful ones, reviewing both houses, my life house and then my business house. Time, effort, and principles are now the only negotiable currency bringing about change. Do your homework first. You decide.

I would like to see our country regain her firm footing. Together it's doable. Unity, recovery, service. No one can do it alone. As my Uncle Abe once said, you cannot pull yourself up by your own bootstraps.

I have personally reclaimed sanity from different forms of degenerative principal practices by practicing regenerative principles in most all my affairs, as a result of my former ignorance, lack of knowledge, lack of understanding, including lack of attention, laziness (mental and physical), lack of discipline, lack of humility, wrongful thinking, and closed-mindedness. I became open to experiment with the regenerative principles by completely giving myself to those principles as best I could, daily remembering that yesterday's practice won't do me any good today. This enlightened, broadened, and deepened my spiritual understand of those principles; their healing effect brought a cleansing and strengthening joy that really support those principles, which produce right thinking, mental balance, emotional stability, and regeneration, physically and spiritually. I have found the principles work for anyone or any collection of individuals, bringing about freedom from want or fear when the principles are adhered to regardless of circumstances. I personally understand the objections produced interiorly within one's self and the objections others have when they say, " It can't be done that way" or " That's too simple, it can't work," which is really a subtle form of dishonesty, and that it has nothing to do with the number of degrees attached to your name, the amount of accolades accumulated in life, or the size and depth of one's pocketbook. I know this for myself from direct experience.

I also spend time at rescue missions helping others and have seen complete restorations. I never gave them bailout money either, not one penny and expected nothing in return. Giving time and teaching by example are greater than giving money and more enlightening. I do give money, however, with full realization that it is only a temporary bandage temporally easing the pain and suffering and that more is required of those capable of change.

This is a story about when I had to choose to place regenerative principles first. Years back I was at an airport drinking coffee, and some individuals (practitioners of the degenerative life powers, principles, or laws), serving their self-interests, approached me and wanted me to fly them somewhere. They would pay me in the neighborhood of a quarter of a million dollars for one roundtrip ride in my plane. A roundtrip commercial ride was $50.00 at the ticket counter. I said sure, why not, and when they left I immediately called a 1 800-BEALERT number. The authorities called me back immediately, telling me to stall those people. We were to leave in about thirty minutes. I said, "You've got to be joking." The authorities said they were in route and would be there in forty-five minutes. I knew whatever those individuals wanted was not talcum powder. The delay worked, and I met the authorities and took them to an attorney friend of mine for proper identification, because these authorities had the power to do whatever they needed to do.

The authorities asked me why I was doing this. I told them it was about time I earned the Good Citizenship merit badge that earned the Eagle Scout award that my mother pinned to my chest when I was thirteen years of age. The authorities asked what these individuals had on me that I would do this. My response was "Nothing."

The authorities said, "We do not understand." I replied, "I am just here to help if you want it," placing what was right and true in the situation. "I'll help any way I can, I just don't want any of my assets confiscated—I've paid all my taxes and I own the plane outright—because something besides talcum powder is probably on board."

The authorities said okay, and I went wired to meet with those individuals. At a meeting planning the trip, someone's beeper went off, and I thought the mike on my chest was backfeeding, and I almost had my first heart attack right there. Authorities wired my plane and something broke. Other arrangements had to be made. I met again with those individuals and made new arrangements, which did not work out.

The head of the authorities called me and said, "We sabotaged the deal on purpose. We have what we need now, thanks to you. If you are ever contacted again by those individuals, just let me know and I'll take care of it. By the way, this was a real deal, involving $83 million dollars worth of drugs."

I'm grateful I was able to help the authorities prevent the distribution of drugs into the veins of our posterity and our children. With regard to the part broken by the authorities on my plane, which I had temporarily forgotten about, two U.S. Treasury agents out of Washington, DC, came to town, called me to meet with me for coffee, and took care of the matter in the proper and correct manner.

My plane is only a tool, not unlike Number 44's plane—only a tool. Mine is not as nice or as modern. Number 44's plane is like a wrench, a very expensive wrench, to tighten down our nation's principles with other nations.

One last story…

I was in a Sunday school class going over *The Sermon on the Mount* by Emit Fox. The minister entered and asked me to come by his office, and I did. He proceeded to pull out a geological map of the Smackover Limestone from his office files and, knowing of my geologic background, wanted my opinion because he wanted to invest in a venture and wanted my expert strata graphic view. As he opened the map and was showing me the prospect, he asked me if it offended me and I replied yes. Extremely so. He immediately put the map back in his files and asked why I was offended. My reply was: "You are the minister to a congregation seeking spiritual guidance in this office, and this is not an office for promoting your selfish personal self-gain purposes. If you want my help, you take the monies you are being paid to be here and go down the street and open another office for these purposes and I will be glad to help you." I was reminded of when

He went into His father's house, turned over a few tables, and vocally kicked some a---- (rear ends). Remember, purity and impurity (anger) don't mix; He was expressing purity of emotions and called them out for acting like harlots. Remember he never harmed anyone ever. The money changers, who are supposed to be there for We the people, are not unlike our sacred halls of Congress in my view. I was never called back, and I am not on his Christmas List either.

I am no minister, and there are many far better and greater men than me. I am only one grain of sand.

By practicing more of the degenerative principles, or laws, than the regenerative principles, or laws, we as individuals and as a nation have been accumulating a spiritual and moral debt that has been building up, which will not be changed one jot or one title, and therefore we reap our just reward, which is the law. Now the bill has come due. If trying to mix the principles in the same manner is continued, the debt *will* continue to increase, and this has nothing to do with money, power, or position being first and everything to do with principles being first. When the principles become first, then the money, power, and position are also healed and leadership is reestablished, called *recovery*. Our nation is the mirror reflecting back our chosen path. As each individual is still good at heart, our nation is still good at heart also. Physician, *heal thyself*, and thy nation shall reflect thy healing in accordance with the law.

I saw on a network show a graph of a red line, a blue line, and a green line, each representing a different party. I think the green line was to represent an Independent Party, which doesn't exist at present. This is what will be needed, which will commit to principle adherence, letting go of old ideas absolutely, having the honesty to recognize the current situation for what it really is and the commitment to change the laws established by old thinking, having an unwavering allegiance to the truth (honesty), and the awakening of faith, yielding to outcome and thereby helping others, We the People, through this process. This new party should begin voting in individuals in the next election and the 2012 election so that whomever We the People choose will have backing in place in the Houses of Congress. No one can do it by themselves. As Uncle Abe once said, You cannot pull your self up by your own bootstraps.

Like I said, a whole new political party needs to come into being based on the regenerative principles, electing practitioners into office in 2010 and 2012. You know, the old thing of not putting new wine in the old wine sacks, especially expecting different results. I would like to see Our Country regain her firm footing. Together it's doable. Unity, recovery, service. No one can do it by themselves. Remember that you cannot pull your own self up by your own boot straps.

I have enjoyed and loved writing this small book as much as I enjoy and love flying. I am grateful to the friends I have met, with charred britches too, who gave this to me. This is merely an attempt to pass it on, and a very poor attempt at best. I'm no communicator or writer. I will admit though, I'm off the merry-go-round now, and I could not have done it by myself.

The family coat of arms symbols: (seen on the back cover) The helmet represents Faith and the Shield Goodwill; the bridge runs over the waters of Honesty, Purity, Unselfishness, and Love (the liquid of liberation) in their three forms, thus the three arches of The Father (of us all), The Son (to us all), The Spirit of Truth (for us all). Trow is an old English word meaning to promise or betroth, and the bridge symbolizes the method to cross over to Liberation. The four different colored plumes atop the Helmet of Faith symbolizes the four regenerative life principles, powers, or laws.

The symbol does not make me a good or great person. I too must be a daily practitioner just like anyone else, to the best of my ability.

Therefore, The Quest, Ancient yet Modern, requires your Piety (devotion) and Fortitude (guts) for Knighthood by Diving into the Liquid of Liberation.

We the people must do it on our own initiative. This is the law. I cannot give another person sanity by my own initiative. I can only convey what to do because someone asked.

Each person has to play the cards they are dealt the way they see fit. With regards to the degenerative practitioners, you could play your personal trump card in your deck by way of your vote - - - YOU'RE FIRED